Harcourt Children's Books is an imprint of Houghton Mifflin Harcourt Publishing Company.

www.hmhbooks.com

The text type was set in Granola. The display type was set in Darkheart.

Library of Congress Cataloging-in-Publication Data
Cyrus, Kurt. The voyage of turtle Rex / written and illustrated by Kurt Cyrus. p. cm. Summary: Follows the life of a giant prehistoric sea turtle. 1. Sea turtles—Juvenile fiction. [1. Stories in rhyme. 2. Sea turtles—Fiction. 3. Turtles—Fiction. 4. Marine animals, Fossil—Fiction. 5. Prehistoric animals—Fiction.] I. Title. PZ8.3.C997Vo 2011
[E]—dc22 · 2010019226

Manufactured in China
LEO 10 9 8 7 6 5 4 3 2 1
4500260448

HARCOURT CHILDREN'S BOOKS
HOUGHTON MIFFLIN HARCOURT
BOSTON   NEW YORK   2011

THE VOYAGE OF TURTLE REX

KURT CYRUS

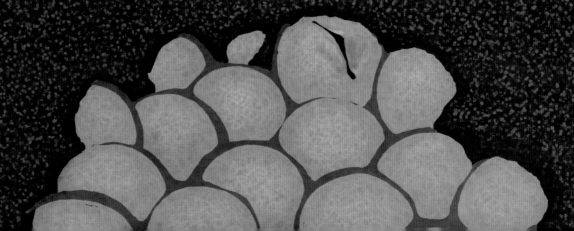

Deep in the dunes of a long-ago shore,

the leathery shell of a turtle egg tore.

Out popped a flipper. Then two. Then four.

They scrabbled and scooped, and scrabbled some more.

The turtle was small. But her flippers were big,

the better to dig with.

Dig! Dig! Dig!

A primeval beach was a spine-tingling sight.

She hid in the sand. She waited for night . . .

or for something enormous to blot out the light.

Then out poured the turtles, a tumble of specks
under the legs of a towering rex.

Sploosh went the waves.

Fizz went the foam.

Swish went the flippers in search of a home.

Rowing ahead into swell after swell,
she teetered and tipped.
She rose.
She fell.
A wave loomed above her. She dove underneath—

and found herself swept through an ocean of teeth.

Surrounded by danger, instinctively rowing,
the turtle kept going
and going
and going.

Into a tangle the sea turtle slipped,

bumping past bladders that bobbed and dipped.

A seaweed hotel! In comfort and style,

a turtle could stay for a long, long while.

Time, like a turtle, passed silently by,

stirring the sea, swirling the sky.

The hatchling who hid in the seaweed was gone . . .

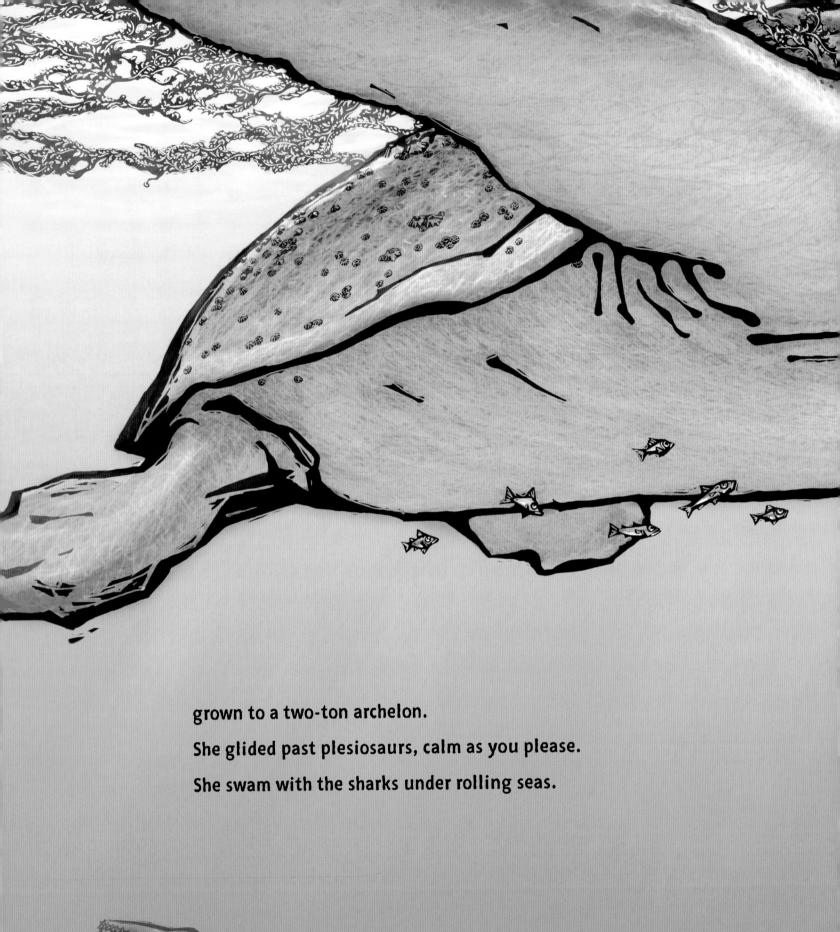

grown to a two-ton archelon.

She glided past plesiosaurs, calm as you please.

She swam with the sharks under rolling seas.

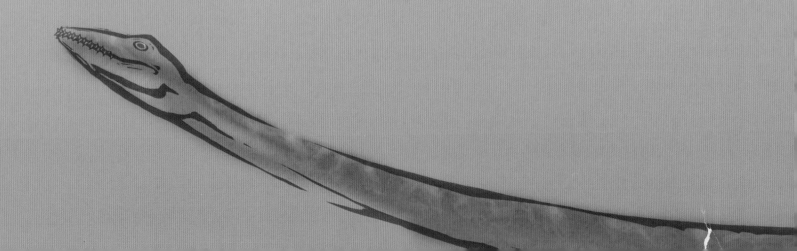

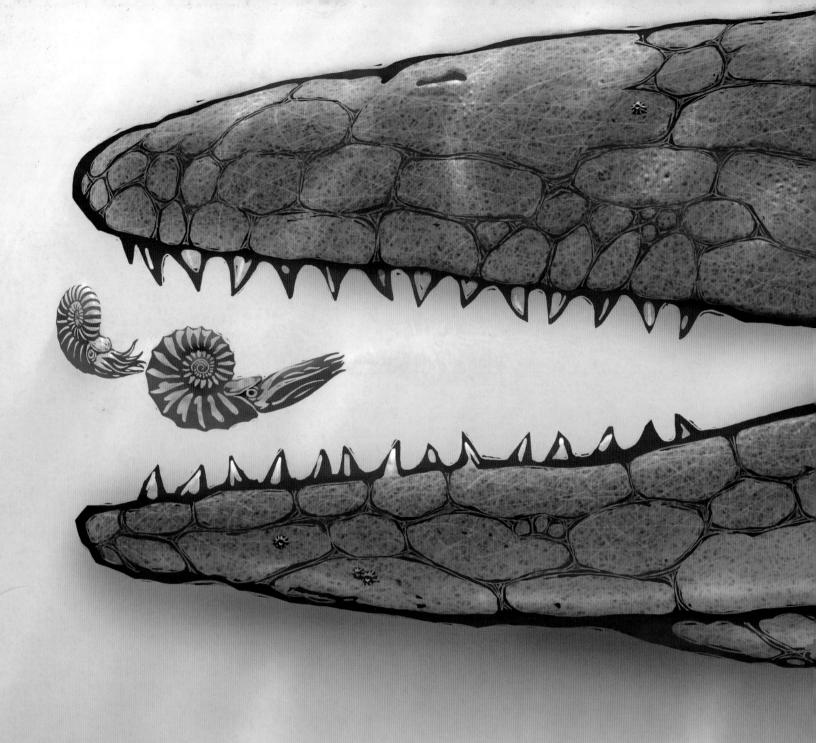

She crossed paths with mosasaur, massive and dark:

muncher of archelon,

gulper of shark.

Quickly she slid to the bottom

and hid.

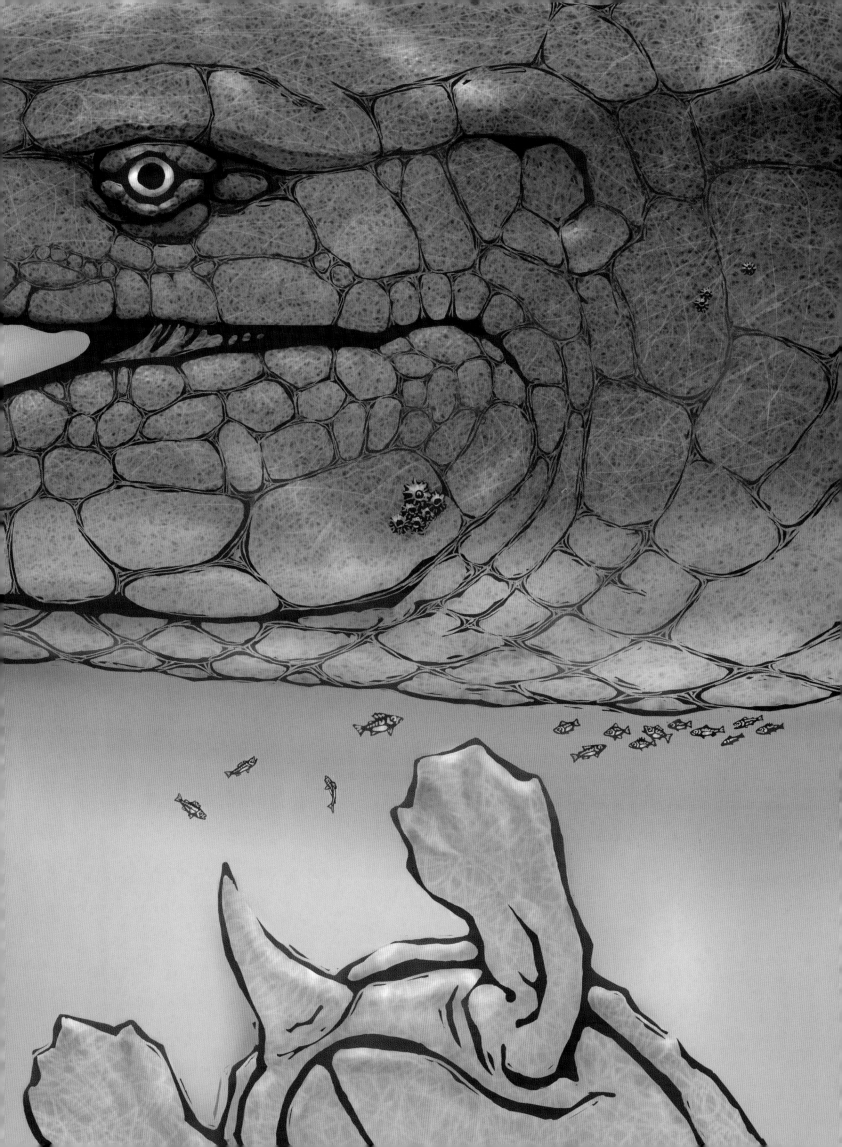

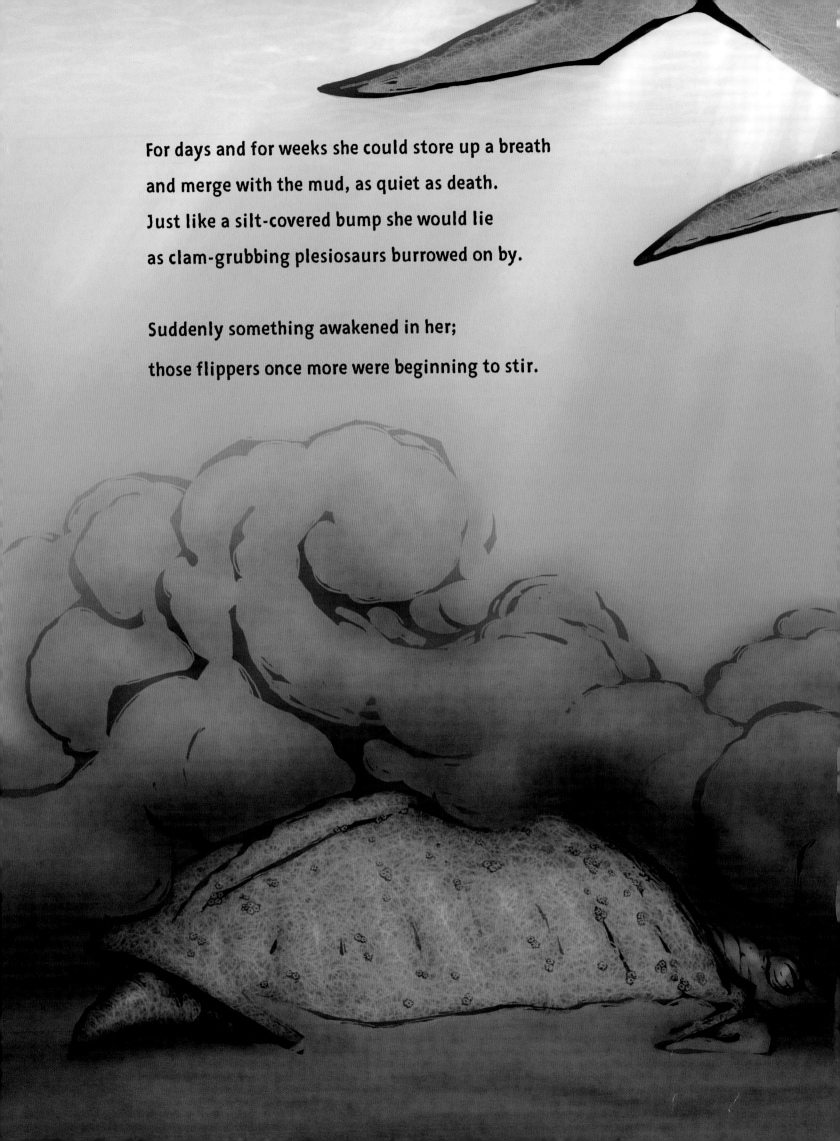

For days and for weeks she could store up a breath
and merge with the mud, as quiet as death.
Just like a silt-covered bump she would lie
as clam-grubbing plesiosaurs burrowed on by.

Suddenly something awakened in her;
those flippers once more were beginning to stir.

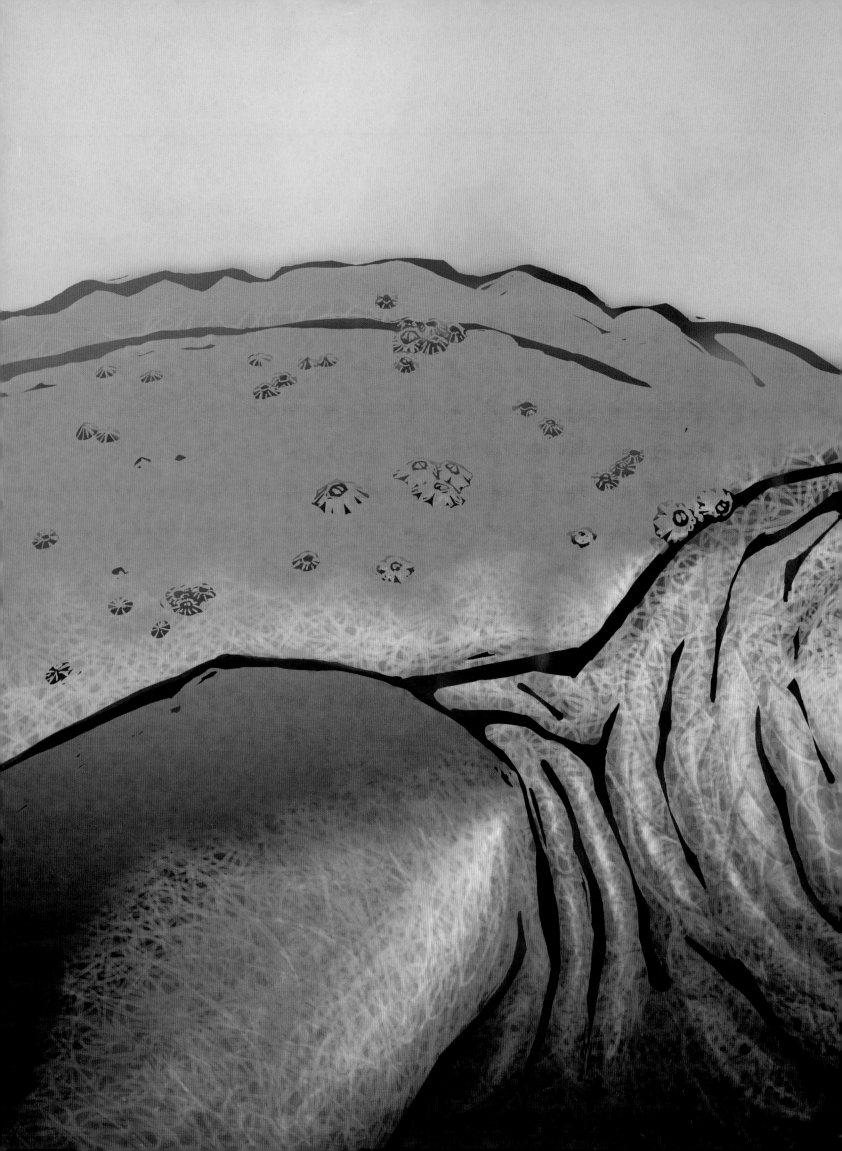

She swung like a compass. Without knowing why,

she left for the land of the sand and sky.

Back to the shallows! Back to the shore!

Back to the world she had fled before.

She swam on a current, she cruised in the sun,
in search of the spot where her life had begun.

Drawn by the hundreds to mingle and breed,

flotillas of archelon swept through the weed.

Crash! went the waves as they broke on the sand.

In slipped the turtle, preparing to land.

She beached in the cool of the evening, and then
her hard-working flippers took over again;
muscular flippers, sturdy and big,
the better to dig with.

Dig! Dig! Dig!

Up flew the sand. Down went the sun.

In dropped her eggs,

and the job was done.

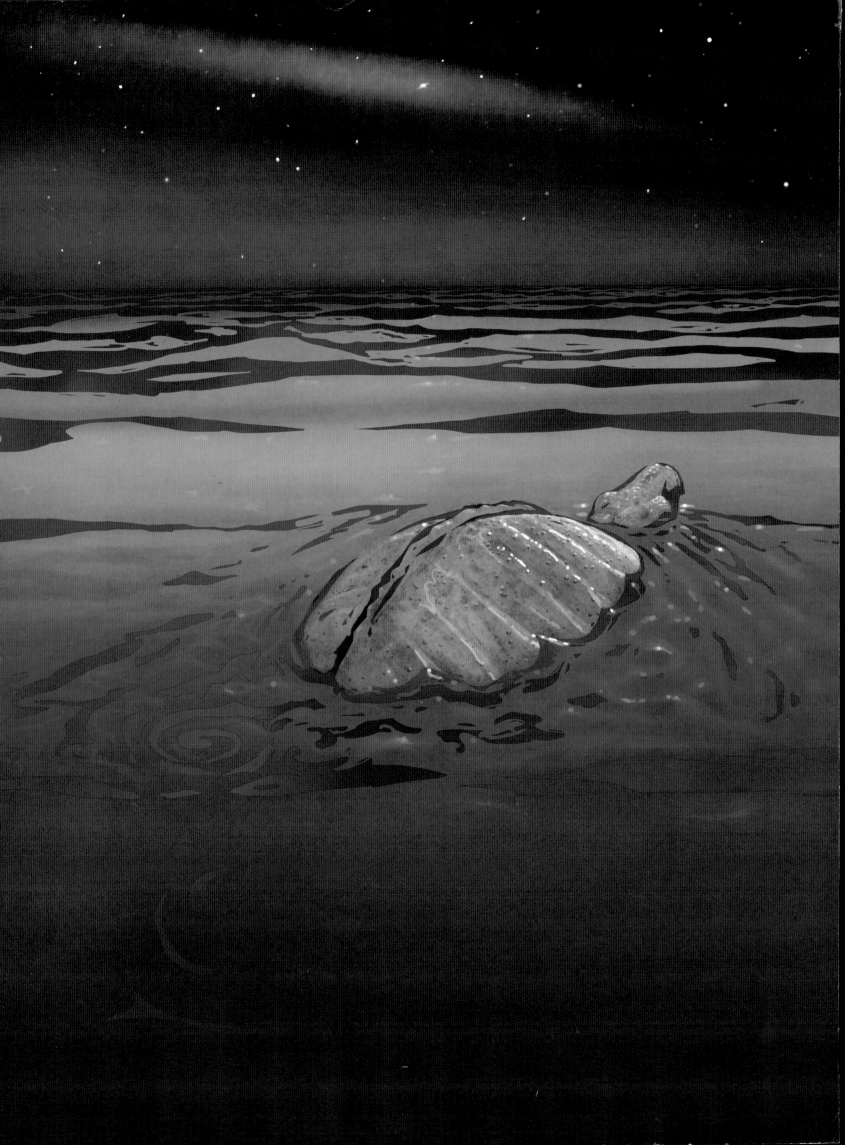

She launched with the tide, exhausted but free
to ripple away on a starlit sea.

Gone is that sea and the creatures it knew.
Archelon. Mosasaur. Pterosaur, too.

Gone is the plesiosaur's clam-cracking smile . . .

but full-body helmets are still in style.

Speckled or spotted, pancake or box;
some soft as leather, some hard as rocks;
shells of all fashions continue to girdle
the middle of many a tortoise and turtle.

And somewhere a sea turtle bolts from the shore,
scraping a trail to the sea once more.

A Note from the Author

Sea turtles in the prairies of Kansas? Sharks in landlocked Manitoba? Yes. Millions of years ago a great seaway covered much of North America. It was in these warm waters that the giant sea turtles swam. Archelon was the biggest turtle species that ever lived. It grew to fifteen feet, about the same size as the enormous white rhinoceros of Africa.

Even though archelon became extinct along with the dinosaurs, seven species of smaller sea turtles exist today. They may not have to dodge dinosaurs or giant marine reptiles, but modern sea turtles face challenges every bit as big. At sea they are accidental victims of commercial fishing. On land their nesting sites are lost to development.

Human activities have put sea turtles in danger of extinction. Now it will take human effort to save them.

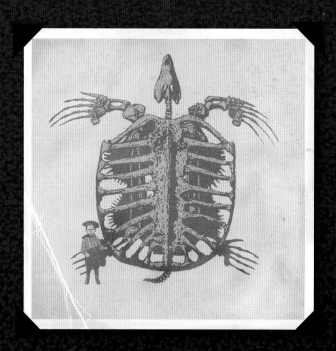

Thanks to Dr. Kraig Derstler of the University of New Orleans for his assistance.